The Wisdom of Beauty

The Wisdom of Beauty

Stephen May

Foreword by Nancy Bauer

Chapel Street Editions

Published by
Chapel Street Editions
Woodstock, New Brunswick
www.chapelstreeteditions.com

Library and Archives Canada Cataloguing in Publication

May, Stephen, 1957-, author

The wisdom of beauty / Stephen May.

ISBN 978-1-988299-17-4 (softcover)

1. Art--Philosophy. I. Title.

N66.M39 2018   700.1   C2018-906114-6

Front cover drawing by Stephen May

Reclining Woman
conté on newsprint, 36 x 24", c. 1980
collection of the artist

Back cover painting by Stephen May

L&A's Garden with Neighbour's House
oil on hardboard, 24 x 24", c. 2010
collection of Claire Ackerman

Book design by Brendan Helmuth

Contents

Foreword

Stephen May and I have been discussing art for many years. He will come unannounced to my door, make us a pot of tea, and we will talk about the wisdom of beauty—with a little family news and general gossip thrown in.

Seven years ago, he emailed me the first draft of this art manifesto. Since then he has been tinkering with it—adding, revising, clarifying, and every once in a while sending me an update. If I were a witness in a trial, I would be able to tell the judge and jury that every single word in this essay is honest and sincere. No posing, no self-aggrandizing mars the essay. He is not pondering the grandiose, not greatness, immortality, or fame; just beauty in its widest sense. This book contains the conclusions Stephen has reached in mid-life after vigorously creating his art for 45 years.

Some artists—and some writers too—regard their practice as hard, difficult work, requiring only sweat and tears. Some regard it as a joke perpetrated on the public. Some think of it as making their lives important, their names known.

But there are those who, like Stephen, do it out of pure joy, with the sense that they might, if they are lucky and faithful, make something wise and valuable to give to the human race. They are encouraged to keep on because every so often, even if rarely, a moment of transcendence appears and announces: "This is good." As Frederick Buechner says, "Vocation is the place where our deep gladness meets the world's deep need."

Stephen and I discuss such questions as "Can a bad person make good art; beautiful, profound art?" We know that a bad man, if handsome and glib, can hoodwink a young woman. Can such a person hoodwink the art public? Or alternately can a good man make bad art, silly or pompous? Stephen and I agree that the making of art—visual or literary or musical—is a sacred trust, a privilege.

At the exhibit of forty-five of May's self-portraits, people tried to interpret his moods. I heard a person say about one painting that he looked disappointed. But as Stephen explained to me, he was not self-psychoanalyzing. He was just using the subject that was near at hand, willing to pose for free—his own face. As he says in this essay, "My best paintings were done by putting dark paint where it looked darkish, light paint where it looked lightish, like some glorified, faulty camera—with two eyes instead of one and self-awareness instead of none."

I have one of his earliest self-portraits, and I've learned to see it as art, not as a selfie photograph. But a mind-boggling complexity occurred when Stephen brought it back to me from the exhibit and said he liked it better on the gallery wall. What had changed?

His painting of a kitchen sink hangs at the end of the table where I regularly sit. When I first purchased it, one woman said, "How can you stand that messy kitchen?" Another woman said, "Ugh; that dirty sink!" It depicts neither—the clean dishes are drying in a rack, the teapot is out to make tea, but the subject is not the point. The point is the arrangement of light and dark, of judicious splashes of colour. It does remind me, however, that writer D. H. Lawrence liked to do dishes, that both poet Brian Bartlett and painter Stephen May are exacting about making their tea. Imagination loves the particular.

In the section "Creativity," Stephen describes how he painted *Dead Trout: Homage to Manet*. A dead trout is not pretty, not like a bouquet of flowers. But Tom Smart, then the curator at the Beaverbrook Art Gallery and now its director, chose to buy it. Recently, curator John Leroux displayed it in the Beaverbrook's permanent Atlantic Canada exhibit. I went to the gallery to figure out why

Stephen himself thinks it's one of his best. Its bold confident brush strokes are breathtaking. The eye of the fish is electric. That much I could tell.

Why does he call it *Homage to Manet*? He has told me a story several times—an iconic moment—of seeing a Manet painting. He had seen several reproductions of *Before the Mirror* and thought it was ho-hum. Then at the Guggenheim he unexpectedly came upon the original and was delighted; "…like the joy and relief you get when an innocent child wanders into the midst of a bunch of pompous grown-ups." Why is he inspired by Manet, Chardin, and Goya? I looked at reproductions of their paintings and got some hints.

I have six of his drawings, three of members of my family, three of me, in graphite pencil, coloured pencil or conté. I pondered why he chose the one of my grandson for an exhibit and not one of the others. What made that one special? The old platitude, "I don't know much about art, but I know what I like" is not good enough for me. I don't want to die not having a clue—and that goes for all the true-hearted accomplishments of the human race. My many hours of talking with Stephen have caused me to look at all art differently. I still am far from "getting it," but at least I now know what I should strive for. I'm glad that Keith Helmuth from Chapel Street Editions heard about the essay and asked Stephen for it so that others can have a similar experience.

Nancy Bauer
Fredericton, New Brunswick
August 2018

So we'll live,
And pray, and sing, and tell old tales, and laugh
At gilded butterflies, and hear poor rogues
Talk of court news, and we'll talk with them too—
Who loses and who wins, who's in, who's out—
And take upon's the mystery of things
As if we were God's spies.

—Shakespeare, *King Lear*

The Wisdom of Beauty

There is no greatness where simplicity, goodness and truth are absent.

−Leo Tolstoy

If you were to look down on Earth from a distance you'd see us doing everything we do. You'd see us following our nature. We do religion and science. We do war and agriculture. We do industry and art. We build tools and organizations. We play. We go from place to place. We learn. We forget. We desire. We reproduce. We die. We ask questions. We argue about the answers.

I had an "Ah ha!" moment a long time ago. It had to do with what I call my job as a painter. I don't mean to justify my paintings. My ambition for them is that they justify themselves. Perhaps I would like to undermine certain assumptions about the power of paintings. They're silent. They won't tell you why they're powerful.

History is a lesson about humans and power. There is something that's very old but never gets old.

– Making it True –

In the late 1800s a critic named G. Albert Aurier reviewed an international exhibition of contemporary art in Brussels that included the work of the Dutch artist Vincent van Gogh. He singled out van Gogh as a leader and praised his work. Van Gogh interpreted that review as praise for the form of his art, praise of the way he used colour. Van Gogh responded with letters to friends and critics. In one of them he wrote, "Aurier's article would encourage me if I dared to let myself go and venture even further, dropping reality and making a kind of music of tones with colour, like some Monticellis. But it's so dear to me, this truth, *trying to make it true*, after all I think, I think, that I would still rather be a shoemaker than a musician in colours."

These words are a confirmation for me. There is something very special and rare in some of his paintings. Van Gogh is not famous because he cut off his ear. Lots of obscure people have hurt themselves. He is famous because of his paintings.

I have an ambition to be a good artist like him. I've painted good paintings and bad paintings. I've spent a lot of time reflecting on my painting experiences. I want to understand what it was that seemed right with me when they were beautiful and what seemed wrong with me when they were banal. My experiences have brought me to an understanding of the way art relates to life, how what is good in art—what is *meant* by good art—relates to what is good in life in general. Goodness doesn't seem to be restricted to particular times or places. It seems to have more to do with the nature of individuals and their relationship to the time and place in which they find themselves.

Beauty is a word. I expect all words came into being to fulfill some need or desire to express something. Some combination of experiences, thoughts, perceptions, and emotions required each of them. Beauty is one of those words with more than one meaning. It fulfills more than one need. It can be a semantics problem that creates misunderstanding between people. I notice I don't always use it the same way. For the purpose of this essay, I mean for it to refer to the good things people do and whatever it is that makes goodness possible.

Artists sometimes say beauty is truth and people sometimes say God is truth or truth is God. That didn't always make sense to me. When the poets John Keats and Emily Dickinson equated beauty with truth, and when Gandhi and Simone Weil said truth is God, I don't think they adopted those words as a kind of slogan for some intellectual position. I think the words occurred to them for the same reason they now make sense to me. I started to understand what they mean when I had my "Ah ha!" moment.

Over the years I've become aware of the difference between truth and falsehood. I have been taught something by all the experiences I've had of finding out that things I was led to believe were true, weren't exactly true. Disillusionment taught me something. I believe I share that with Keats, Dickinson and others who equate beauty with truth.

Disillusionment can lead us to see illusion for what it is. I get terribly discouraged now when I see the abuse of illusion, when I see illusion being held up as truth, illusion used to placate, control, or exploit. Even when illusion is merely meant to entertain it has a seductive quality. People can use it to nurture a taste for escapism, which can become a need. The temptation to exploit that need is powerful. When we accept the abuse of illusion we set ourselves up for disillusionment.

We allow ourselves to be exploitable. Our taste for fantastic tales, romantic myths, and false proofs is dangerous. Our susceptibility to propaganda and flattering hierarchies is dangerous. If truth is dressed up to suit us, everything gets worse. Disillusionment leaves us sour. My problem was how to pass through disillusionment and emerge undefeated.

Simone Weil describes prayer as paying attention. I thought I stopped praying when I was a teenager but now I think perhaps I've continued to pray all along.

The "Ah ha!" moment I referred to happened in my last year in the fine arts program, at Mount Allison University in 1982. I was painting a self-portrait while looking in the mirror. It was progressing in a way typical for me at that time. I was thinking about other people's paintings. I was thinking of the various styles, skills and techniques I could make use of. The painting was progressing in a self-conscious and imitative way. I noticed that and became frustrated with it.

At the same time, I realized the painting didn't look like what I saw in the mirror. In that moment of frustration I made a few energetic slashes with dark paint to reconnect the painting with what I saw in the mirror. The painting turned a corner. It suddenly had some kind of authenticity it didn't have a few moments earlier. It doesn't sound like much to relate, but the proverbial light bulb came on. *Pay attention! It's right there! It's always right there, waiting.*

Painting is an act. Painting is living just like all the other acts we find ourselves involved in. The problem of painting—the problem of whether to paint or not, how to paint, what to paint—is the same problem we all face in just being human. It's the problem of figuring out what to do with one's life, to figure out what is possible. A person acts and we find out what is possible. Shakespeare wrote plays.

Life's but a walking shadow, a poor player, that struts and frets his hour upon the stage and then is heard no more; it is a tale told by an idiot, full of sound and fury, signifying nothing.

–Shakespeare

However it may have come to pass, a man, an artist like Shakespeare was possible. We want some explanation for his power and the continued effect his art has on us. The only thing we can see and hear is the form. We're tempted to look for the secret there. We look for Shakespeare's formula or the formula *of* Shakespeare, for the social/psychological reality of the man in his time and place. We look for the formulas' of Bach, George Eliot, Manet, Joni Mitchell, Gandhi, Nelson Mandela. We long to know what allows some people to leave us better off than we would have been without them. Those who do that are invariably un-secretive (though often silent) and the infinite variety of the forms their actions take suggests that it's something very un-formula-like at the root of it. The root of whatever it takes to do something good outside the art world might be the same as within it.

The lines above are from Shakespeare's play *Macbeth* and are spoken by the character Macbeth. They are Shakespeare's profound expression of the emptiness a man is left with after a particular kind of failure. Macbeth is a play about people (Macbeth and Lady Macbeth) who failed miserably to do good things. It's a tale of ego driven ambition.

Our ego lives behind our eyes; it feeds on the energy of the world and uses that energy to build illusions within us. Those illusions become so powerful we have trouble seeing anything else. Bitter disillusionment arrives when the truth of things eventually forces its way through that blind of illusions. The Macbeth characters in Shakespeare's play were blinded like that and suffered for it. Shakespeare, however, was not blind.

A beautiful painting is never simple. It's never just some canvas with colours on it, never just the image and what it may or may not symbolize, never just an artist's diary or an artist's tastes and opinions, and never just a reflection of the artist's culture. We all tend to be distracted by the specifics of our life, our passions, etc. Art usually ends up just being about those specifics. It ends up just being about our identity, our culture, our economic reality, our tastes, our ideas, our bloated selves.

– Truth –

The only true wisdom is knowing you know nothing.

–Socrates

Emily Dickinson said that her country was truth. I feel the same way. I think of truth as everything that is, whatever it is. Truth is. It's a borderless country. We're always home.

As the word "diamond" is a name for something real, the word "truth" is a name for something real. A name for a thing is never the thing itself.

Knowledge is something different than truth. The nature of truth and the nature of knowledge stand in sharp contrast. There is a crucial distinction between the two that we often fail to make. "Knowledge" is the word we use to refer to things we are certain of. "Truth" is the word that refers to something the nature of which we should never be certain.

The scientific knowledge we possess is sometimes called provisional, as in, we know such and such, provided it doesn't turn out to be proven un-true. Referring to scientific knowledge in that way amounts to an acknowledgment that there is a crucial difference between knowledge and truth.

The knowledge some people possess that has to do with their faith, amounts to a claim of certainty about something that is un-provable. Many (most?) people don't seem to make a distinction between knowledge and truth.

People crave certainty. We want there to be something sure, something solid, something we can stand on that won't shift around. When I hear a person say, "I know,"

I understand them to mean they're certain about something. Or sometimes they seem to be trying to convince themselves their certainty about something is justified. If faith can be said to have different strengths, a person who says, "I know," is expressing the strongest faith one can have. Even the strongest faith is susceptible to doubt. Knowledge is susceptible to doubt. It's rare that there is any *absolute* justification for any of our particular certainties, for any knowledge.

Knowledge is fragile. It changes. It disappears. Truth abides. If all knowledge ceased to exist, truth would remain. When the sun goes nova and the biological incident on this Earth ends, and there's no more knowing, truth will abide. Knowledge is a kind of human possession. It feels like a solid material thing. Because our nature requires certainty, possessing knowledge makes us more comfortable. We are un-comfortable with our inability to possess truth.

I see the garden in the Bible's *Book of Genesis* as a metaphor for a possible relationship to truth. The story of the expulsion from the Garden is about a characteristic of our nature that undermines the wise relationship to truth. The story is about our love of knowledge over truth, our love of material certainty over uncertainty.

There is a strong sexual element in the story. It amounts to a male voice (the authors of the Bible) accusing the female nature of too great an attachment to the material world. This ironically serves to demonstrate the powerful grasp that the material world has on all of us, regardless of, or maybe *because* of, identity. We're all biased towards the material reality of our own bodies. The different and distinct biological identities of both men and women often result in behaviour that is hard to understand and love. Living outside the Garden, we live outside love.

A material garden is an illusion. Garden is a word. It's a name. The thing itself, like anything itself, is infinite (if William Blake is right). Most of what is actually there in what we consider to be a material garden has to be unseen for us to think of it as a garden. Truth is unruly. It includes weeds and snakes.

The story of Eve and Adam eating the fruit of the tree of the knowledge of good and evil describes the moment we adopt in our minds the supremacy of our tastes and opinions. It describes the moment we decide that there is something wrong with truth, something wrong with weeds and snakes, something wrong with God. It's the moment we *know* (are certain) that there is good and evil. It's the moment we *know* which is which. It's the birth of relativism and materialism within us, the birth of the idea that it's for us to determine the nature of the Garden, for us to judge as gods. We transform truth into what we know.

I am the way and the truth and the life.
–John 14:6.

The Christ story can be taken as a metaphor for a wise relationship to truth. Christ can be understood as truth embodied in the material world (incarnation). Salvation becomes ours by way of loving Christ, loving God, loving truth. Salvation is a return to the Garden. I can interpret Christian wisdom as a particular relationship to the world, a way of living by which we return to the Garden. I see the Garden not in the realm of hopes and dreams, but in the realm of the real and present, the realm of the tangible and tactile. It's the realm of artists like Emily Dickinson. The world we make and inhabit becomes a world of love. There is no greater Garden, real or imagined.

The facts and Faiths of each historical age have been different from the preceding ages. If we respect truth, there is very little we have a right to be certain of beyond the fact that truth is. When I hear myself saying "I am" or "I feel," I can't doubt that I am and that I feel. Almost everything else is speculation. But I don't know what being and feeling ultimately are.

Am I my consciousness? Is my consciousness a web of neurons firing in the gray matter of the brain? Am I that plus the rest of what is called an organism, my tissues, my bones, my fingernails, and hair? Do I become somebody else if I stop showering and turn my body into a host for a greater microcosm of bacteria? Am I the information stored in my genes? Do I become immortal if I pass it on to my children, extinct if I don't? Am I my experiences, my memories of them? Am I the thing psychologists call *ego*, which I imagine as a flattering picture painted by my consciousness to represent me to myself, like the picture I have of other people, only more important? Am I as infinite and eternal as truth or an insignificant blip?

I can't doubt that I am, but I can doubt any claim about my true nature. I can't doubt that there is something other than me, but I can doubt any claim about the true nature of whatever is other than me.

A painter of pictures is confronted by questions. What does this painting I'm doing have to do with me? What does this scene have to do with this painting? What do I have to do with this scene? If we respect truth, if we decide to love truth and are determined to search for it, our Holy Grail won't exactly be an object. What is wonderful about art is how that love of truth, that search, becomes manifest in our objects and actions. The absence of prejudice becomes solid. Anything justly sacred in life grows out of a determination to love truth. What is embodied in some of van Gogh's paintings has become justly sacred.

– Faith and Reason –

"… and at once it struck me what quality went to form a Man of Achievement, especially in Literature, and which Shakespeare possessed so enormously—I mean Negative Capability, that is, when a man is capable of being in

uncertainties, mysteries, doubts, without any irritable reaching after fact and reason…"

–John Keats

We are reasoning beings, but reason is limited. Consciousness is faced with that limit, faced with how unreasonable existence is. Einstein said there are only two ways to look at the world; either nothing is a miracle or everything is a miracle. In some quarters, reason is understood to be the one method by which we have a right to claim certainty. My reasoning, though, brings me to my ultimate absence of certainty. Socrates' statement about true wisdom means the path of reason is the path to uncertainty. We are both rational and irrational beings. These aspects of our nature work together. My rational nature, my reason, forces me to be uncertain. My irrational nature, my faith and instinct allow me to act effectively, to act with conviction, in the absence of certainty. My irrational nature allows reason to empower my action.

Even science, which is thought of as a purely rational pursuit, is actually an irrational one; it grew out of the irrational part of our nature. It's questionable whether science and technology, as human activities, are any wiser pursuits than anything else we do. It's a quagmire trying to decide if and how to regulate or limit them. Ages ago, when our ancestors began to exercise the part of human nature that resulted in the invention of science, they couldn't have known the profound effect it would have on the world. There is little doubt that knowledge is power and that science puts power in our hands. But it's also rational to realize we can't know where this power will take us, rational to doubt the wisdom of humans becoming more powerful. Rationally we are forced to be uncertain about it.

Any reasonable person should question the wisdom of an absolute faith in painting. Any reasonable person should question the wisdom of an absolute faith in a personal God.

Any reasonable person should question an absolute faith in science and technology.

We can't know the future our actions will bring or the complexity of how they will affect the world. We tend to do what we do because we can, because we're good at it, and because we like or need to do it. It's human behavior. If at some point we're challenged to examine what we do, we look for a way to rationalize it.

All our pursuits are irrational. If we examine our actions closely we can recognize faith and instinct at their root. People have to *believe* in the point of building cathedrals and particle colliders. We have to believe in a tomorrow for ourselves that we can't see.

But, we also rely on reason. It's a powerful tool. We have great faith in it. It's a faith that can become so profound that it makes asking reasonable questions about the limits of reason seem unreasonable. We are powerfully compelled to stay within reason. But any reasonable person should question an absolute faith in reason. My absolute faith in reason is destroyed when faced with the question of why there is possibility instead of the absence of possibility. Possibility following the absence of possibility is absurd. Existence (possibility) is without explanation. The reason to ask *why* is to confront the limits of reason. It's unreasonable to ask *how*. I can't deal with the fact of existence in the rational way I can deal with nature. I'm forced to use a word like miracle.

– This Cave is Brilliant –

We're inside a room. And the room is inside the truth. We gaze out the window or step outside and the outside is no longer outside but still within the room. Looking and stepping are of the room. We forever remain in the room. Though the walls appear to expand without limit, the room never changes size. The room is word-sized. The room is number-sized. The room is image-sized. The room is time-sized. All our subjectivity and objectivity are in the room. We build a telescope and the room accommodates a particular and relatively large past. We build a particle collider and the room accommodates a particular and relatively small present. We gaze into our mind and the limit of all experience and reason are the walls of the room.

The walls of the room have no colour. They have no darkness or lightness. They have no heat or coolness, no texture, no solidity, no airiness, no thickness or transparency. All physics is of the room. All imagination is of the room. The absence of quality is what holds us eternally within a mystery, a mystery that reason and objectivity are powerless to dispel.

There is no image, no metaphor, and no language that is not the room. We experience the shivers of experience and the blow of understanding the impossibility of understanding. We reveal nothing. We speak only words and by the words are revealed. We are of truth. We are by truth. We are truth and all our philosophy and art, our religion and science are us and truth revealed. I am. Truth is. Not a word. Not a word. It's a terrible blow to the writer's pride, the painter's pride, the scientist's pride, the bishop's pride, and to the understanding of knowledge as justified certainty. It destroys pride.

"Creation" and "infinity" are easy words to say, but they are non-answers. What we call proof dissolves into wisps of possibility and probability. What we call knowledge is not the same as truth. We "know" things today we will "know" aren't true tomorrow. People in different times and places have expressed their realization that the truth is not ours to know. This realization comes in the form of warnings in the Bible against presuming God's reasons, in Plato's cave analogy, and in Buddhist koans. It's beyond our ken. We can't reason it out. This realization is what Socrates calls wisdom. I know truth is, but I mustn't presume its nature. To say "all is illusion" is no relief from my profound perplexity. The word "is" remains. The word "is" haunts me.

The best use of words like "God" and "truth" is to acknowledge shattered pride and reason. There is less danger, however, in presuming the nature of the word "truth" than in presuming the nature of the word "God." When we use "God," it's hard to avoid equating mystery with something like lord or father or mother, with love or anger, with creative or nurturing power, with something we can understand. Mystery is moved in the direction of non-mystery and we undermine its significance. We undermine the psychic weight of mystery. We undermine the real significance of the word "God."

Rationally we are forced into a confrontation with the irrational. "Infinity," "creation," and "illusion" are all words used to replace our absence of understanding with the comfort of symbols. *Something* rather than *nothing* is an uncomfortable absurdity that's hard to face. In math class we learned that division by zero is undefined. We represent the un-definable, the absurd result, with an infinity symbol.

– What to Do? –

I wake every morning faced with reality. I must live without certainty and understanding. I live and then I die. How do I decide what to do with this life that is inexplicably thrust upon me? I cannot consider myself to be absolutely free to do as I please. I see that other people, other entities, are inevitably made miserable by my actions. We always leave footprints. Things we don't see are under each footfall.

People who act as if they are absolutely free don't consider their footfalls. The more we act that way, the more we become the pariahs (as individuals, classes or cultures) in the worlds of other entities. We become perceived as the evil that needs to be defeated. If ants hate, they would probably be justified in hating us. Our Western culture is an indulgent culture, condemned and/or envied by others. We leave very big footprints.

This problem underlies the whole of human history. The idea that goodness is relative is too often taken as a license for a person to do whatever makes them happy. It's an idea that is interpreted as sanctioning indulgence and turning a blind eye to the miseries caused by our indulgent behaviour. This is a world full of miseries. If we look closely we will see ourselves complicit in more miseries than we want to know about. All actions have consequences. The more we act, the greater the effect of our lives and the greater the consequences on the world around us.

It's a lie to claim we are free, to claim that freedom is not chained to responsibility. I find the ideology of relative goodness to be unacceptable. Something compels me to try and understand goodness in some other way. Goodness has to be something free of the imperious nature of ideology. It's a struggle to avoid ideology. I find myself rolling down into it. The process of thinking seems to be steeply inclined in that direction.

Something in my life experience has led me to the understanding that goodness is generated by loving truth. As John Keats discovered, it's the one thing to know. Being driven to love truth occurred naturally and spontaneously for me, but it's counterintuitive at the same time. There is much about the way things are that we would change if we could. Keats died a painful death of tuberculosis when he was only twenty-five. Simone Weil was a French Jewish refuge of Nazism who had to put up with chronic bad headaches and died, for puzzling reasons, from starvation. These were their lives; yet, they were compelled to love truth.

Personally, I've had little to complain about. For me, this loving truth, this relationship between truth and beauty has not been a trial by fire. On the other hand, I'm quite certain I will die soon. I'm quite certain that all I am, all I've done, and everyone I love and care about will soon be dust, forgotten on this earth.

Keats believed that people are able to transcend intellectual and social conventions and creatively exceed what is normally regarded as the constraints of human nature. He's not alone in his belief in transcendence. But, in being determined to love truth, I can't let myself be absolutely certain that transcendence in art happens. I can't let myself be certain that the whole becomes greater than the sum of the parts. It's possible that I see what I want to see and believe what I want to believe.

When the French painter Manet offers his advice, "If it's there, it's there. If not, start over," I want this to be his acknowledgment of transcendence. I want his word "it" to refer to transcendence. He might have meant something else, but I see evidence that a painting can transcend its time and place, transcend the class and identity of its maker—evidence, but no proof. I can't be sure that it's not just my buttons being pushed when I find I love Manet's art, when I find myself loving the art of some other distant time and place, some other culture. The truth may be that I am merely a bio-chemical machine, a beast that is stimulated in pleasant and unpleasant ways.

It's clear, however, that there are exceptional people in all areas of human endeavour, people who do and make exceptional things. There are the Michael Jordans, the Nikola Teslas, the Wangari Maathais and the Warren Buffetts of the world. Different circumstances and personal characteristics were at the root of how each of them was able to be exceptional; such factors must also be at the root of how certain artists are able to be exceptional. There is a power source. What was the source of Keats' or Dickinson's power? I keep being reintroduced to a power while painting. I keep being instructed to love. I get a powerful sense of material reality being transformed by that love. I feel like I've entered a different country.

If I'm just a bio-chemical machine and transcendence is a romantic notion, then I must be prepared to love that reality and that love will empower me. If God is three-persons and there are angels and devils, heaven, hell, limbo and purgatory, then I must be prepared to love that and that love will empower me. But I don't know any of those things and I don't know how to know them. I am at sea. I will love that I'm at sea and that love empowers me. I don't know why it empowers me, but it does. My relationship to the world is transformed. My affect on the world is transformed. My paintings get better. My relationship to others is transformed. A love of truth moves me towards accepting others, in spite of not being able to understand them. It's like truth is leading me to love truth; it's a weird, positive, "catch-22" situation.

– Fall on Your Knees –

To act as if I had sure knowledge, to paint as if I knew what I was doing, as if knowledge was truth, would be a first selfish act, a first subjective act that sanctions all subsequent selfish acts. It would be the end of wisdom. It would be the end of loving truth. It would be the end of true love. It would be the beginning of simplistic childishness. It would be the beginning of the sanctioning of all acts of relative good. It would be the end of beautiful action. It would be the end of beauty in my life. I wouldn't want to paint anymore.

"Truth is beauty is God." This is an unreasonable statement, a useless statement unless you can define at least one of the words. Such a statement means the person who makes it claims no sure knowledge. In the poem where Keats claims that beauty is truth his next and crucial words are, "that is all ye know." This is a different articulation of Socrates' wisdom. Such a statement acknowledges that the person who made it has fallen on their knees.

The palpable answer to the question of what the expression *beauty is truth* means is Bach, Beethoven, van Gogh, Manet, Rembrandt, Nelson Mandela, Gandhi, Simone Weil, Tolstoy, Shakespeare, George Eliot, Dr. King Jr. and Socrates. The answer is the things they've done. It's the beautiful things that each of us—if we've been lucky—has directly experienced other people doing, whether those things have been recorded as history or not. Heaven, at least, can be other people.

In her book, *Gravity and Grace*, Simone Weil gives us an apt analogy. She describes how loving truth works in terms of a space that is normally filled up with self, a space filled up with reason, passion, and imagination. Only if we can remove our self from that space—she used the expression "de-create" the self—will there be room for beauty or truth or God to arrive, which she calls "grace."

We tend to fill up that space with loyalties to countries other than truth. We fill it up with loyalties to humanism or Catholicism, to socialism or capitalism, to democracy or monarchies, to our families or our nation, to our peers. We fill it up with a loyalty to our self.

T.S. Eliot shares Weil's understanding of the state of being that makes human goodness possible, in his case, a good poet. In *The Sacred Wood* he writes, "The progress of an artist is a continual self-sacrifice, a continual extinction of personality." Likewise, James Joyce, in *Portrait of the Artist as a Young Man*, gives these words to Stephen Daedalus; "The personality of the artist, at first a cry or a cadence or a mood and then a fluid and lambent narrative, finally refines itself out of existence, impersonalizes itself so, to speak." A few lines later he writes; "The artist, like the God of the creation, remains within or behind or beyond or above his handiwork, invisible, refined out of existence, indifferent, paring his fingernails."

Shakespeare lived and worked in London in the Elizabethan age, along with other playwrights. Was he displaying his personality or was his personality absent when writing plays?

I think whatever might be called wisdom, whether in science, religion, philosophy, art or anything else in life must begin with what could be called loving truth. No matter what the field of endeavour, if it's undertaken with awareness, faith is involved. I am not, strictly speaking, a religious man, but there seems to be little separation for me now between art and religion, painting and prayer, beauty, truth, and God. Or at least little separation between how those things can be wise and good. If you consider aesthetics as a philosophy of art, then for me aesthetics and ethics have merged. I'm not surprised to find that beauty is universal like the golden rule.

My experience has led me to become a slave to truth. We are all slaves to something. We are slaves to our biology, to sex, hunger, and the need for sleep. Our Western culture makes us slaves to the ideology of freedom. It may be that we are free in some situations to choose what we will be slaves to. I've found only one form of slavery that brings me freedom—slavery to truth. It's the one slavery that delivers me from the idea of a slave and master relationship.

It's probably wrong to call it slavery. If the self can be de-created, then that leaves no oppressor and nothing to be oppressed. But maybe it's necessary for the first few steps on a path back to the Garden to be the steps of a slave or servant. Perhaps that humility is a required condition on the way to exaltation. Dr. Martin Luther King Jr. said the only freedom is from the love of wealth and the fear of death.

Truth is, but I don't know its nature. My best paintings were done by putting dark paint where it looked darkish, light paint where it looked lightish, like some glorified, faulty camera—with two eyes instead of one and self-awareness instead of none. Perhaps it's a quest akin to some Olympian trying to be the fastest man when any mutt dog could outrun him. Cezanne said derogatorily of Monet that he was "only an eye—yet what an eye!"

I love Monet's late paintings of the Japanese footbridge, when cataracts had ruined his eyes.

When I go to an art gallery, I'm searching for something and am compelled to walk away when it doesn't appear to be present. If I can separate the good from the not so good, the difference between them becomes much clearer. The success of this phenomenon might be why there are long line-ups to get into the Musée D'Orsay every day, why some people become well-known and loved, if they happen to have made things that last a little while.

– The Brothel of Illustration –

I was once taken aback by the comments of a teacher to a group of teens in the Metropolitan Museum of Art in New York while standing in front of Manet's *Young Lady in 1866*. The teacher suggested to the kids that it wasn't beautiful and they seemed to agree. To me, it was a beautiful painting. I was left to wonder if they were focusing on the face of the woman portrayed, which is quite plain. A beautiful painting is not a representation of something you think is beautiful.

If you see an image of an attractive and healthy young man or woman, or a sympathetic portrait of a beloved personality, a saint for instance, or an image of some idyllic setting, a place you'd like to be in, you have to be extremely wary. All of us involved in art have to make ourselves aware of the seductive power of imagery. Art so often fails to be more than expressions of taste or pandering to taste. Art very often fails to be more than seduction, manipulation or of special interest.

The only way we know beauty is by seeing it or hearing it, by feeling it. We can be fooled. In the end beauty is what something *is* and not what it looks like.

My struggle to come to terms with experience is the same as anyone's. We all arrive innocent and unaware. We're raised on illusions and comforted by them.

My moments of disillusionment were unpleasant and life changing. I found out that things weren't what they looked like, what I was led to believe they were. People can be taught the dangers of mistaking illusion for truth through experience. Some people, however, learn to wear blinkers their whole lives, loving illusion. Some learn to be cynical and don intellectual armour.

In spite of guidebooks, everybody faces this dilemma alone. We keep trying to pass on the wisdom we have gained from experience but it never seems to work. An old commandment, an old wisdom such as "Thou shalt make no graven image," doesn't make much sense to us. But if we make images of God from imagination, in words or pictures, and then love those images, it's really ourselves that we love. We create God in our image. We get what we want. We enter the brothel of illustration. It seems experience is the only way we truly learn anything. In part, I learned by painting.

Mythology (someone else's religion), imagination, and ideas are such powerful realities. They are like warm blankets. But blankets are insular. We can live within them comfortably at a distance from truth. The danger is that one person's blanket, one person's cherished ideas or particular cultural myths, will inevitably be different from another's. Fear and hate are born in this difference and comfort ends. Prejudice grows.

There is an attraction to the intellect for its own sake, to rhetoric and sophistry. Rhetoric is dangerous. It's a truly ugly idea that if you're better at rhetoric than anyone else in the room, you win and truth is yours. However, it's possible to use intelligence to safeguard against cleverness and distinguish the difference between truth and rhetoric. It takes integrity and vigilance to avoid banality and its attendant evils, the comforting, placating, controlling and exploitive powers of well-spun illusions.

– Beauty as Success –

We have a habit of debasing words, using them indiscriminately. For the word "beauty" not to become a victim of that tendency we have to use it to refer to something other than opinion. We are not, each of us, our own fascist dictators of beauty. If that were the case beauty wouldn't matter and the word may as well remain debased. It could only be a joke to claim that opinions or particular tastes will save the world. Wherever humans are involved, beauty is likely to wear the hat of taste, the shirt of sentiment, the pants of opinion, the shoes of concept, or the gloves of skill. But its essence is something other, something without which all those things are empty gestures and only lie about in an interesting heap.

Beauty, for me, at least as it relates to human activity, is a measure of a certain kind of success; not an anti-materialistic success, but definitely a non-materialistic success. It's the success of loving disinterestedly, the results of how you behave when you love without consideration of personal gain.

I think it's reasonable to claim that disinterested love, manifested in anything we do, regardless of whether on an historical or non-historical scale, is the greatest human accomplishment. It's the success of an unprejudiced acceptance of what exists, what is true. It's the true absence of prejudice. Beauty, in these terms, empowers us to trust in human goodness and can give us the faith to endeavour to be good ourselves.

Art is greatest when it's beautiful. I think it's a necessarily generous, un-grandiose, and un-guarded activity. It's very difficult to keep your successes from going to your head. The transcendence that is apparent in art might be a transcendence of pretentiousness, a transcendence of pride. If there is one thing we can unequivocally celebrate and rejoice in, it's our ability to be beautiful. Beauty is life rewarding life. It's our one meaningful legacy, ephemeral as it is.

– Art and Consequence –

The word "art" is like the word "beauty;" many different people understand both in many different ways. Art is another semantics problem. I've noticed a fashion in today's art world for subversive art—art that must subvert accepted notions of value in order to be of value. It can lead to subversion for subversion's sake. It has become the strategy of certain ironic artists to try to subvert notions of the value and meaning of art itself. The reason-for-being for this kind of art is to undermine its reason-for-being. I find this kind of activity disingenuous if not entirely hypocritical and vain. It seems like such a purposeful waste of resources. It's the manifestation of another aspect of human nature I have great difficulty loving.

When I first started making art I didn't question the point of art. I was excited about what I was doing. It was obvious that good art had been made and that I might be able to make it too. Later I encountered art that disconcerted me. I encountered serious art, art that made it into art history books, art that left me puzzled about other artists' understanding of the nature of art. For example, I found it hard to accept anti-art as art.

I eventually realized that it's pointless arguing about whether something is art or not. I also came to notice that all the art I've encountered, regardless of whether I think it's good or bad, has something in common. I've adopted a practical, working definition of art based on this common factor. I now understand art as a phenomenon inseparable from being human. I understand art as the phenomenon where you encounter the maker in the thing made, the doer in the thing done.

For instance, when I encounter the documentation in an art history book of a man (an artist) pointing at a horse and calling it a work of art, I notice and accept that nothing has changed with respect to the horse, it's still whatever a horse is, but rather my mind has been affected by another human's (the artist's) mind. The art phenomenon happened. My puzzlement was the consequence of encountering his art.

This definition of art as a physical phenomenon is inclusive. Humans and the phenomenon of art go together as do mass and the phenomenon of gravity. Where there is human presence, art is present. We leave traces. The phenomenon has unavoidable consequences that can be perceived as good or bad for the particular humans involved. Any limited definition of art such as *art is politics* is true and not true. Politics is art (the art phenomenon is present and we can see the artist/politician in his art/politics) but not all art is politics. Beautiful painting is art but not all art is beautiful painting. An articulated idea is art but not all art is articulated idea.

Some people involved in art believe that art is idea. I say *articulated* idea because an idea by itself cannot really be considered art. The idea that idea itself is art came from the early twentieth century Western art movement called Dada. Dada was an absurdist branch of surrealism that, in some instances, manifested itself as anti-art. I believe the purpose of anti-art is to subvert notions of the possible values of art. It could be understood as a protest against materialism. I believe the movement was a reaction/response to the pointless horrors of the World Wars and the vanities of the art world and the world in general. It was a time when general disillusionment was understandably widespread (disillusionment is always a threat).

The French-born Dada artist Marcel Duchamp was eventually led to make the claim that art is idea. His statement amounts to the ultimate flag of surrender in face of the futility of trying to *make* anti-art. As long as he *made* or *did* or *said* anything he discovered that the art phenomenon arrived. His attempts to escape the nature of art, the phenomenon of art, the value of art were frustrated. He discovered that anti-art *is* art.

Duchamp's anti-art art, like any art, can't avoid the value of the art phenomenon and I think he recognized this. Idea is *not* art, but his *statement* that art is idea *is* art. The statement is Duchamp's ultimate work of anti-art. It's the statement we encounter, the statement that has consequences. Duchamp eventually stopped making art and spent his time playing chess instead. I can respect that choice given his convictions. Sometimes I feel like I'd like to quit painting and just play hockey. But nobody would pay me to play hockey.

The material reality of anti-art has consequences. It teaches you about people who make or do or say anti-art things. If Duchamp's anti-art is understood as a protest against materialism it can influence a person into adopting a misguided anti-materialist ideology. Being anti-materialist is foolish. Whatever the mysterious nature of material is, we are it. If you pay money to enter an art gallery to encounter a work of art protesting perceived materialist/capitalist ideology, or when you're asked to pay money to own that work of art, the situation is ironic, whether intentionally or not. The artist and/or gallery expect to benefit in material ways—food, fame, grants, a more impressive C.V., etc. It's a cynical or hypocritical act. Things turn sour. It makes an empty fashion of protest-art.

Ideas happen in your head. Everything else happens somewhere else. Ideas are the only things small enough to fit in your head. Ideas are something other than art. They are imperfectly manifested in art. They must be embodied in some way in order to be encountered as art, in order to *be* art. Without the *art* part ideas are un-encountered, un-affecting and without consequence. Un-articulated or un-embodied ideas can't be found in art history books or art galleries or on the street.

As gravity is tied to mass, art is tied to what people make and do. Art is where we come face to face with our inevitable and ambivalent relationship to physical things, the footprints we make and the noises we hear. Art is a phenomenon that is as real as anything else. Art is not the un-real among the real. An artist who thinks of art as unreal is weakened by that idea.

In this respect, it's not the phenomenon itself we're fascinated by, that we have such positive or negative responses to, but rather the individuals and cultures revealed by the phenomenon. The art phenomenon is the only way we become aware of other people. The power of the artist comes from the realization that physical reality is the only way we can make connections with anyone else. The connections are not perfect. What we see and hear is open to interpretation. None-the-less other people are truly there in the art.

I don't consider the imperfection of those connections to be a license for me to indulge in a personal interpretation of what other people do and therefore who they might be.

I consider it my responsibility to pay attention and seek out who is truly there. I'm often not up to that responsibility but I feel I only make myself poorer by an indulgence in interpretation and do a disservice to the other person at the same time.

I wouldn't call a person an artist who doesn't wish to be called an artist. I wouldn't deny any person's claim to be an artist. People who would never have called themselves artists made a substantial percentage of the objects that are found in general art history books. Those objects are included because they reveal something noteworthy about the people who made them. It could be that people who have an instinct to reveal themselves to the world are the ones who tend to call themselves artists.

The following words by dancer Mikhail Baryshnikov ring true for me. "When a dancer comes onstage, he is not just a blank slate that the choreographer has written on. Behind him he has all the decisions he has made in his life…each time, he has chosen, and in what he is onstage you see the result of those choices. You are looking at the person he is, the person who, at this point, he cannot help but be.… Exceptional dancers, in my experience, are also exceptional people, people with an *attitude* toward life, a kind of quest, and an internal quality. They know who they are, and they show this to you, willingly."

To be called or not called an artist doesn't matter. The phenomenon is unavoidable.

As we are, so art is. Art can be what *we* can be. If we can be good, art can be good. Art can be bad. Art can be mediocre. The question of what is mysteriously good about some art remains. This question is why we can't leave art alone. This question is inseparable from what is mysteriously good about some people.

There are many ways in which art is considered to be good, some cynical and some not cynical. Art has been considered good if it's extraordinarily expensive, extraordinarily famous, extraordinarily memorable, extraordinarily pleasant or unpleasant, extraordinarily skilful, or if it requires extraordinary resources to achieve. Art has been considered good if it's intellectually engaging, perceived as innovative, or critical of human behaviour. Art has been considered good if it undermines or alters your understanding of art, is therapeutic for the artist, or is understood to be imaginative or creative. Art that shows humans to a proud advantage has been considered good. Art has been considered good if it asks hard questions.

With this inclusive understanding of art-as-phenomenon we can't presume that our difficult questions will be answered by art. We can't presume that our lives will be made better by art. Our lives are often made much worse by art. Art in these terms is something of unquestionable consequence. For instance, the things a mediocre or malevolent air traffic controller might do or neglect to do will have real consequences. A malevolent person is a malevolent person. A mediocre artist is a mediocre artist. Shakespeare and Bach stand apart from mediocrity. Nelson Mandela and Einstein stand apart from mediocrity. But so too does Stalin. They are exceptional people. There are significant, palpable, real consequences to art.

– The Consequences of Beauty –

Art has also been considered good if it's beautiful. That is what I believe in and work towards as an artist. This has been called a relativistic age. Relativists will charge a person who claims a close relationship with the absolute to be absolutist. The claim that beauty is truth is then suspect. A human attempting to make beauty in those terms must be an absolutist. I understand absolutism as claiming to possess knowledge of the absolute truth and claiming absolute authority to impose it on others.

Beauty involves loving truth. That's a very different relationship to the absolute than claiming to know the absolute. My relationship to truth has made it apparent to me how little absolute knowledge I possess. The more beautiful a person becomes, the farther away they are from being absolutist. One has only to compare the words and deeds of people such as Stalin and Hitler with Ghandi and Nelson Mandela to see the difference. Absolutism is all about imposition and control. Beauty is open acceptance. It's true love.

Most of the time painters impose their will on their canvases. Rembrandt did many paintings of wilful self-expression. He did paintings that displayed his extraordinary skill and ones where he likely flattered his patrons. But his self-portrait in the collection of the Kenwood House in London manifests open acceptance. Strategy is absent in that painting. Being strategic is only necessary if you're not intuitive about being beautiful.

Loving life might be the only true wisdom. I have trouble loving life sometimes, trouble loving many of the worlds within life. I have trouble loving the art world, for instance.

One of the parts of life I do love is when people's actions aren't motivated by self-interest. I believe that if my art ever seems to be a truly good thing, the roots of that goodness lie in my desire to act without self-interest. That desire is ultimately mysterious to me. It might even be considered pathological if it's understood as a mental state that isn't normal, and ultimately unhealthy for the person who suffers from it—the starving artist, the martyr.

Early on in my painting experience I discovered that my paintings got better if I exchanged a desire for knowledge and skill about painting with a desire to be truthful about everything. Since then I've discovered that self-interest is the great barrier to being truthful. Through experience, I discovered you can't first love yourself and only then love truth. It doesn't work. Beautiful painting doesn't happen. I don't think anything good, anything beautiful in the world, happens unless you can remove self-interest.

We should never be too sure that a thing is beautiful. It would be a comforting certainty. The music of Mozart is often referred to as a trustworthy example of beauty. I've mentioned the names of a number of exceptional people whose art I feel confident about. Mozart was certainly an exceptional person, but I haven't mentioned Mozart because I am usually irritated by his music. I hear too much flippancy in his music, as if he doesn't respect his audience, doesn't respect me. I do, however, hear wonderful things in the midst of it. I find myself wishing he'd been more consistently sincere. I have to doubt my qualifications to judge his art.

Beauty has no pope. It might be that I fail to respond to Mozart's art because it pushes particular buttons that happen to irritate me. I might love the artists I love because we share the same tastes. Much of Gordon Lightfoot's music is beautiful to me. Other people don't find it so. Maybe it isn't possible for a person to be beautiful as I understand beauty.

Maybe true selflessness isn't possible. Maybe it isn't possible for a human to be a super-conductor of truth. Maybe there will always be the resistance of reason and passion.

If we never know, we must always be learning. I might, in time, learn to get over my objections to Mozart. I don't know if I *want* to get over the un-felt conventions of form that a lack of artistic vigilance allows. The consequences of the phenomenon of beauty, of being beautiful, are inseparable from the consequences of the absence of being self-serving, the absence of the tendency to be absolutist. Any step away from beauty is the greatest danger we face.

– Creativity –

The imagination is continually at work filling up all the fissures through which grace might pass.

–Simone Weil, *Gravity and Grace*

Many people assume that an artist is creative. It's considered an enviable quality to possess. I've had a running debate with myself about creativity. I'm not sure what we call creativity in humans is really something to brag about. If it is, I'm not sure if I can claim to be a creative artist among artists. I compare what I do as an artist to what some other artists do and I wonder if I'm just a monkey compared to someone like Bach—something like the way Cezanne felt about Monet. My paintings are representational. Bach's music is abstract. I don't know where great music comes from. Perhaps he was creative and I'm not.

At 10 a.m. one summer day in 1991 I stood in front of a large blank canvas. By 5 p.m. a painting existed which I consider to be one of the best things I've ever done as an artist (*Dead Trout: Homage to Manet*). The painting is not what I'd imagined it would be, not what I was trying to do. I know I made decisions as I was painting it. Some of them were based on my tastes and ideas. Some of them weren't. I was led.

It isn't an arbitrary painting. It's definitely related to that actual fish I bought at the store earlier that day. I would like to know where the painting came from.

A long time ago, the Rocky Mountains weren't there; then the tectonic plates shifted and now they are. Birds, fish and ants build things and rearrange their surroundings. Bowerbird's bowers weren't there and then they are. My fish painting wasn't there and then it was. It's not what I wanted it to be. It's good in a way that I never imagined or intended. I don't think we would say the tectonic plates imagined or intended the Rockies. I don't know what the real root of these new things is. I don't know whether creation is a proper word to account for them. I don't want to risk losing whatever it is that allows me to make paintings like the one of the fish. An arrogant presumption of creativity might put that at risk. It's true that nobody else painted my painting. It *was* Chardin that painted a copper water cistern after all. It was Monet that painted a field of grass.

Painters, and people who talk about painting, use the word "greys" to refer to the tints and tones, the little in-between colours that aren't quite this and aren't quite that. People acknowledge that those greys are what make some of Chardin's and Monet's painting so special. What passes through the fissures?

Leonard Cohen said something to the effect that he didn't write his songs but he's really glad we think he did. I've heard other artists express that same idea. I wonder if Bach considered himself to be a creative person. I think I've heard that he devoted everything he did to God. Is that his acknowledgment of the fortunate artist's grace? Some people might insist I'm creative, others might insist I'm not. I'm uncomfortable with the claim.

I've also become ambivalent about the word "imagination". It typically refers to something understood to be the root of human creativity. But in one sense, Weil is right about it. The root of the word "imagination" is "image." Our minds are filled with a collection of images. We mash images and make fantastic monstrosities, brain excrement. We squeeze stuff out to fill up movies and books and pictures and it stinks of indulgence. We're proud of it like a toddler proud of his stool. When the word is used that way I don't want anything to do with it.

On the other hand, if it wasn't for Weil's ability to connect experiences, if it wasn't for her memory, if it wasn't for her consciousness of the connectedness of the whole of her accumulated experience to the experience of the moment, she could never have strung those words together. Perhaps that crucial connecting process would be a better way to understand imagination. Bach has some mysterious way of stringing notes together. In E.M. Forester's novel *Howard's End* he offers his commandment, "Only connect!"

It's a novel about the troubles of the world caused by people who lack imagination.

The word "feeling" in art presents me with a similar problem. In a romantic sense, feeling seems to be understood to be various emotions manufactured within the artist and broadcast outwards, emotions for emotion's sake. But when I use the word I mean something more like empathy. The antennae on roofs and the feelers on bugs are apparatus for real things to cross a threshold and become apparent.

Many artists only use their skills to play with ideas and images. The images in paintings can be read as a set of symbols, skillfully delivered ideas, or representations of images from the artist's imagination. The ideas, or the images and their associations, will appeal to you or they won't. That is their limit. Some artists only play with illusion, like magicians, but when you find out how it was done the magic disappears; you gain nothing by moving up close to it or remaining with it for hours.

On the other hand, some art rewards closeness. Alchemy is the old, mystical, and suspect art whereby non-precious material is turned into precious material. In painting a kind of alchemy is possible. By way of the alchemy of feeling, beauty is temporarily recoverable. Lucian Freud's alchemy recovered what Chardin's alchemy recovered what Rembrandt's alchemy recovered. It's essentially the same alchemy and the same thing being recovered. Some painters instinctively understand that. We tend to know their names. That alchemy doesn't happen when painting is strictly an intellectual or technical or sentimental pursuit. The presence of that alchemy in painting is a crucial element in early Modern Art that often gets overlooked. It's the life in painting.

There are paintings that become more literally wonderful the closer we get to them. Getting closer to them we enter a field of limitless wonder. I can't feel lonely when I'm with some particular Chardin paintings. I have never gotten to be in a room with someone like Gandhi or the Dalai Lama but I wouldn't be surprised if, in some crucial way, the experience would be akin to that of being in the room with a Chardin painting.

We see the other and define ourselves by our separateness. Our ego creates the separateness: the Occident and the Orient, the Stone Age person and the astronaut, the believers and the atheists, all the sexes and non-sexes, life and non-life, all of however many universes there might be. Our painting efforts are all directed towards de-creating (Weil's expression) the separateness our ego creates—trying to become un-blind to the universal in the specific. We fail and we succeed.

Cezanne said, "I should like to astonish Paris with an apple." As with Chardin's and Manet's, his paintings of apples continue to astonish. It doesn't take much imagination to put an apple in front of you in order to paint a picture of it. We can't imagine beauty. We can only connect. We can only be beautiful. We can only be graced.

– Elements of Art –

If it's there, it's there. If not, start over.

–Manet

The elements of art are form, media and content. All that art is or could be is accommodated by those terms. When I think about beauty in art and try to analyze its nature in terms of those three elements I start to get confused. Beauty doesn't seem to be properly accommodated by any one of them. I can either hold on to a clear definition of each element or the definitions of each begin to expand to accommodate beauty and I'm no longer able to understand each element distinctly. The whole enterprise becomes like an expanding cloud for me. It could just be a deficiency of intelligence on my part.

– Form –

Art always takes a form, but the form art takes isn't what matters in art. If an artist's goal is to find new forms or to conserve old forms the essential point is being missed.

Tradition and innovation are not ends. The orthodox story of progressive Western Art has it that the painters Manet and Picasso are remarkable for breaking old forms and inventing new ones. Really, though, they are remarkable because they're good, just like van Gogh. One painter's form is smooth and another's rough. Rembrandt's rough form can be found in Titian. It's not innovation that is remarkable about Rembrandt. Good art takes form out of the precinct of words. Those who find refuge in form, the progressive and conservative alike, never escape history, never escape their own time. Oscar Wilde asks us to be kind to fashion because it dies so young. I can't muster much sympathy.

Manet's contemporaries were offended by what they saw as his lack of respect for what they considered to be the serious concerns of art. Things don't change much. We get so caught up in ideas of the moment. His early paintings strike me as signposts, as if he is saying, "You want to understand what I'm doing?—look at Velazquez."

The idea of progress creates the idea of obsolescence. Manet's art however is not obsolete. It makes most subsequent painting look like window dressing and doodles. It makes most of his contemporaries' paintings look like huge bags of brownish wind. I've often had the thought that Masaccio and his contemporaries (proto-Renaissance artists) and Manet (the proto-Impressionist artist) taught their respective generations of painters to start looking again, to start paying attention again.

Manet could be called a realist painter. The word "realist" has different meanings but sometimes when people associate themselves with the word it reveals their desire to dismantle false hierarchies. It's meant to express a willingness to accept all that is experienced, even though it may undermine romantic/idealist notions of our place in the universe. There have been many painters willing to put us in our place but few who have done so with such gentle humour, intelligence and kind sympathy as Manet. They say you should never meet your heroes but the more I read about him the more endearing I find him. His close friend and fellow artist Berthe Morisot wrote about him in a letter: "Poor Manet is sad. His exhibits are, as usual, not to the taste of the public—a perpetual source of surprise to him."

One of the remarkable things about Manet that took people by surprise was his radical acceptance of his medium. In his finished works bits of white canvas are left bare and certain details are rendered by a few obvious, economical brush strokes, like in Chinese Chan or Japanese Zen painting and Rembrandt's brush drawings. You'd get the same sense of the artists' acceptance of the medium if you were in the Lascaux or Chauvet caves. There would be no danger of mistaking the stonewalls for anything other than stonewalls. They don't let the general public into those caves anymore for conservation reasons. They have built a life-size model for people to visit. The "stone" is probably fiberglass. That's a different kind of art by different kind of people, for a different purpose.

Drawing and painting from life can help artists escape their identity. Manet's models complained of many long sittings, which is probably why they all look so bored. Van Gogh's piercing look in his self-portraits is what he saw in the mirror. It's the look that anyone who posed for him would have seen on his face. It's the look of a man paying fierce attention.

The art of the Canadian painter Tom Thomson was pretty corny when he wasn't confronting his landscape directly. Monet built a big new studio in order to paint his huge panoramic water lily paintings. They came from a very different place artistically than when he took a canvas down to the actual pond. They don't fill me with awe like some of his work does. When the water lily paintings were first installed in The Orangerie in Paris, a critic said they looked like decorations in a first class cabin on an ocean liner. To me they look like Monet's imagination, his concept got the better of him.

Monet, Thomson, Manet, and van Gogh were all compelled to work from life. They didn't work exclusively from life, but it was a continual and crucial practice for them. I've worked almost exclusively from life ever since my "Ah ha!" moment. It can be a frustrating practice. It severely restricts my subject matter. It's a restriction I'm willing to accept. I'm rewarded for it in ways I value more than the rewards I'd get if I indulged my thinking.

Manet was reported to have said that a painter can say all he needs to say with fruit or flowers or even clouds. The unremarkable becomes remarkable.

Chardin claims to use colours but to paint with feeling. His tiny painting of a copper water cistern and ladle embarrasses much of the hugely ambitious and sophisticated art with which it shares space in the Louvre. Sophistication can lead away from goodness.

Van Gogh stuck candles to his hat so he could see what he was doing when he painted outside at night. Marcel Duchamp called that kind of painting stupid. Duchamp expressed his cynicism about the value of painting when he marked up a print of the *Mona Lisa* with a drawn-on moustache and a risqué quip at the bottom. Van Gogh painted *The Café Terrace at Night*. The sublime and the ridiculous are sometimes Siamese twins. If you don't mind looking ridiculous with candles on your hat, the sublime may be attainable. Our passions make fools of us. A passion for beauty, however, makes you do whatever it takes to end up selfless and disinterested.

The American abstract expressionist painters Joan Mitchell and Jackson Pollock didn't work from life as I do. Neither did the cave artists. They found the source that provides the strength of their art by some other path. It's always easy for painters to lose touch with their source. Pollock had periods when he was out of touch with his source. Any time I move away from the source—and it happens against my will—I can see my personal idiosyncrasies being repeated and my art growing tedious. It's almost normal for me to be unable to find my way back to the source again on any given day. Still, I know it's there.

What is it exactly that painters are feeling, and where can we rely on finding it? How does it pass through us? I don't want to assume Mitchell and Pollock understood good painting in the same way I do. I'm sure they noticed a difference between their good paintings and bad paintings. They knew when they had to keep going and when they could stop. There is a huge Mitchell painting in the National Gallery in Washington that I would call beautiful. It was hung right around the corner from a Pollock painting that requires some adjective that denotes the exceptionally good. We find, we learn, we lose, we learn, we find, we learn.

– Media –

A medium—the physical stuff we manipulate that other people experience with their five (or more?) senses that let them know the manipulator exists: the coloured earth-pigments rubbed on stonewalls; the little black squiggles marked on white paper or backlit screens; the things we make vibrate that change the way the air and light vibrates; the heat and pressure and chemicals we generate.

The old-style social media are vibrating vocal chords, body language and the pressure of body part on body part. They are perfume and body odour. They are food and hugs and kisses and how they taste and feel.

The new social and artistic media are vibrating vocal chords and body images in electronic transformations. They are microphones and cameras. They are keypads and transmitted little black squiggles and fingers pressed against screens. They are flat video screens of various sizes and speakers.

Our different physiologies determines whether a medium is personally suitable or not. Mozart's physiology included a brain with a phenomenal memory for complex series of sounds. There is an anecdote of him hearing a concerto performed once and then going home and writing the music down for each instrument. If his physiology hadn't allowed for that, he would likely have needed to find a different way to express himself, a medium other than musical composition. If I didn't have working eyes I would have needed to find a medium other than painting. That has nothing to do whether the art is good or not.

The relationship between artist and medium is more complex than that. An artist who is able to give us something wonderful in one medium won't necessarily be able to offer something wonderful in another medium. As artists, we can recognize when something special happens in our art and can have an instinctual understanding of why or how. But we can find ourselves frustrated from manifesting that specialness in all media by something in our individual natures. Michelangelo wrote poems and Joni Mitchell made paintings. They aren't particularly noteworthy.

I sing and play the guitar. My vocal chords and a guitar are media for my artistic expression. Sometimes it sounds OK to me when I play other people's songs, but I've tried many times to write songs and it's clear to me how much they leave to be desired. I'm confident to show my paintings but I'm embarrassed to play the songs I have written when others are listening. They are like Michelangelo's poems and Joni Mitchell's paintings.

My voice has a limited range and not great tone. My fingers don't move very fast which puts a frustrating limit on my guitar playing. My brain can't seem to grasp the complexity of great music. I have a poor memory for notes.

Physiology delivers and restricts opportunities for exceptionally good art.

If we have something to contribute, something to say, we are fortunate if we can find or invent a medium that suits us. Beyond that, an obsession with media is just that. We are the message. Our potential is the medium's potential. The truth within Marshall McLuhan's claim that "the medium is the message" is the truth of a cultural numbness that can grow as a medium grows. Love and empathy can easily disappear within a medium's increasing complexity. Any new medium will deliver our instinctual egoism—deliver our tedious idiosyncrasies—just as well as the old ones. Broader, quicker dissemination of those things is no great comfort. Some media are more and some less ephemeral, but they all eventually melt into air.

Painting as a medium persists because it's obvious and infinitely supple. An artist can't hide behind painting. It eventually becomes obvious whether "it's there" or not (as Manet says) and when it *is* there, the painting pulls us back to experience it again.

Media have great powers to persuade and we are subject to a powerful social instinct to conform. I've heard people speak of this era as the information age. The internet can be understood as a huge collective art work. Some people see the internet in an idealistic way; see it coming to contain the total of human knowledge, universally accessible. They see the possibility of it delivering all of humanity to a utopia of collective intelligence. Information, intelligence and wisdom are different things.

The internet is obviously powerful. It will form our thoughts and actions and move us in directions we aren't aware of and that aren't necessarily good for us, or for the world we share with everything else. We like the warm bath (McLuhan's metaphor). But it's full of soap scum and our own dead skin cells. The bathtub itself is going somewhere we might not appreciate when we get there. The road back might have us naked and out in the bitter cold—history tells us that's a distinct possibility. Tommy Lee

Jones' character in the original *Men in Black* movie said, "A person is smart. People are stupid." (Ed Solomon, screenwriter). The force of mob psychology grows with the size of the mob. The internet is huge and growing. See the old newsreels of a whole nation of ordinary people like you and I, ecstatic about a lunatic. See a coliseum packed with ordinary people like you and I, thrilling to lions eating people. See what we're doing now? Not really.

Powerful media power popular movements. There is a tradition of artists, and others seeking wisdom, sequestering themselves. It's a way to resist the tides of mass movement and popular thought.

– Content –

When someone talks about the content of a work of art they're usually referring to what the artist meant for the work to communicate—or to what they *think* the artist meant to communicate. Content usually means what the art is *about*. If an artist choreographs a ballet-style pas de deux (the form) for live dancers (the medium) about faded love, then the artist's take on faded love is considered to be the content.

If that is truly the extent of content in art, then content alone won't determine the quality of the performance. Content, by that definition of the word, would be a constant in each performance of the dance, yet some performances would inevitably be better than others. A more expansive understanding of content is required. Content is more complex than just what the art is about.

Whenever something gets formed—by humans or otherwise—all the obvious and the unfathomable causes of its being formed are *contained* within it. Content could refer to all that is contained in the form, all that courses through the medium, independent of our ability to understand it. It could refer to the whole of the nature of the artist in the world. The true content of art is the complex nature of people facing the complex nature of the world.

Art doesn't need to be *about* consequential matters in order to be of consequence. Art's great value is not as illustration or documentation or story or metaphor, but as the embodiment of what we are. Imagery and symbols come naturally to painting which can lead one to believe that is the content limit of painting. Twentieth-century painters abandoned the image to declare a kinship with music's intrinsic abstract qualities. The same is true in modern dance and literature that abandons plot. The motivation to dispense with certain things that seem to be superfluous is understandable. However, there are no formal safeguards against failing to be beautiful, no formulas for achieving it. Art without images or plots can be just as banal as art with images or plots.

Images have an innate treachery to mislead. However, when we see, when we feel with our eyes, it happens in colour patches, in light and dark shapes. Illusions are created in our heads that relate directly to something outside our heads, the awareness of which has profound influence on us. We respond in all the ways humans have always responded ever since we've been human; we back away, we approach in fear, in wonderment. A response while painting—while making those colour patches, those dark and light shapes on the canvas—can innocently turn those head-illusions into images corresponding to what we see.

A culture turns images into symbols that have meaning only for that culture. However, if there are a thousand paintings of flowers, each can operate perfectly well as symbols for flowers. Each can communicate "flowers" to anyone of that culture, anyone who can read the language of those symbols. Some few of those thousand paintings of flowers may be beautiful paintings. The treachery of the image is that it distracts you from realizing that the essence of a painting isn't the visible image, the essence is the embodied artist.

For every painter who feels as Rembrandt felt (and they are rare), there are thousands of painters whose symbols are the same as Rembrandt's. For every painter who feels as Tom Thomson felt (in his plein-air sketches), there are thousands of painters whose symbols are the same as Thomson's. There was no choice for Rembrandt and Thomson. Their paintings must look the way they do. We will always be faced with piercing illusion in search of truth.

> *There is nothing new under the sun.*
>
> – Ecclesiastes 1:9

Van Gogh and his brother Theo were very close. Theo wrote to their sister Wilhelmien about the experiences he had living with his brother and about their conversations on art and life. The following is an excerpt from one of Theo's letters to her that seems to reflect Vincent's thinking: "He [Vincent] is one of the avant-garde for new ideas, that is to say, there is nothing new under the sun and so it would be better to say for the regeneration of old ideas which through routine have been diluted and worn out."

There are new things of course, but all they offer us are new platforms on which to manifest the same successes and failures of old. "I am." "I am not the only thing." Consciousness is. Truth is. There is no *new* human condition. The Great Mystery abides.

Within consciousness there is but acceptance and assertion. There is the baby and the bath water. Beauty becomes obscured in the bath water of new ideas. Our ideas become entrenched and turn into ideology and frozen doctrine. The understanding that ideas are the content of art is a narrow one. Art-as-idea itself is a frozen doctrine. Nothing good happens when ideas replace feeling. Visual artists who are strict idealists are confined to illustrating their tenets. Plato didn't think much of painting. But then who knows what he would have thought of painting if he'd gotten to see Manet's or van Gogh's paintings, if he'd gotten to see the paintings of animals in the Chauvet or Lascaux caves.

There are differences of opinion about what governs our actions. There is little point in claiming a determining role for chance, fate or freewill in art. Chance, fate, providence, determinism, and freewill are all perceptions, the truth of which eludes us. Holding to one or the other is ideology, with ideology's attendant dangers.

Institutions—academies for instance—are typically defined by the ideas their members have of their institution. They are inevitably drawn into their own ideologies and away from feeling. This phenomenon is how the adjective "academic" became a derogatory one in the art world. That phenomenon is happening now, no less than in the nineteenth century. If there are still humans in the future, it will happen then too. They will be indoctrinated into new academies just as people were in the past and are now.

What we always notice is difference. We notice differences between cynicism and sincerity, between selfishness and generosity, between cruelty and kindness. The explanations that academic art come to require will never replace what is missing in the art.

There is nothing new about what matters. Manet was no more Modern than Jesus was Catholic. People remark on how "modern" some of the 40,000 year old drawings in the Chauvet and Lascaux caves look. The baby is always there to be found. Sometimes artists find it when they're making art. Great art is always radical, of the root.

The history of what matters is more like a pulse than a march. What we hold eternally valuable becomes embodied in the forms of the day. It's eternally valuable because there is no "us" without it. Though some marks on cave walls only say "I was here", others are more mysterious. Though Baroque music is an old form, Bach's compositions will not grow old. They keep teaching each new generation what they are. I don't really care what art is about; I haven't for a long time. If I can't make my art true, it's going to be empty no matter what it's about.

– Communion –

A number of years ago I was thinking about the commodification of art, about the forces that pressure artists like me to sell out. I ended up with these words: *There is always a conflict between art as communion and art as commodity. Fortunately, when you are painting, you can forget that it will become a product and it can end up having a value that is different from money.*

There is an important distinction between art as communication and art as communion. In cases where an artist has a limited understanding of art as communication, the opportunities and positive rewards of communion are not intended. The artist is unconscious of the greatest potential of art.

Their art is likely to leave you with only a negative reward of communion. It will likely only take your time and energy and attention. Often you can read a few paragraphs about that kind of art and you will get all there is to get out of it. You can save yourself a trip to an art gallery.

A person goes into a forest to commune with nature. Cities have been called works of art. People are drawn to Paris and New York for their energy. When people arrive in a place, they change the energy. You enter a city and become part of it. Our nature is embodied in our art. Beautiful art embodies a generous nature. We commune with the nature of the artist. You don't need to own the art. You just need to see it or hear it or taste it. You don't need to own a forest to benefit by being in it. Nobody really owns a forest. Nobody owns nature. Nobody owns gravity. Nobody owns the art phenomenon. The claims of ownership are illusions. It's all one big communion. We show respect for communion in the way we treat things (art objects for example). We belong to something.

– I Have My Moments –

Van Gogh wrote about how the blank canvas tells you you're stupid and you can't do anything. That doesn't necessarily end once you've put some paint on it. It can keep going for hours, days, weeks. The painting scoffs at you. The painting rolls its eyes with contempt for what you are doing. The painting says "Beauty is truth? Yeah, right. Idiot!" The painting keeps torturing you with the news that everything is empty and pointless. The painting in front of you makes you feel like what you're doing is irrelevant, a ridiculous pursuit for an able-bodied intelligent man.

All artists make things that aren't beautiful. Sometimes some of them make things that are beautiful. Making beautiful things is beyond me. If it were just a matter of sincere faith and desire, I would only ever make beautiful things. I feel more fortunate than accomplished when it happens. Simone Weil talks about waiting for God.

Sometimes I feel like I've gained access to a spring. What is wonderful is the sense I have that it's unlimited. It will give me whatever I can carry away. All I need to do is to collect some of it. My creative ego, the place where my fears live, just feels itself to be stupid and becomes nothing.

If the doors of perception were cleansed every thing would appear to man as it is, infinite.

–William Blake

As the best musicians listen, so the best painters look.

When I started out as a painter, I emulated my heroes in a superficial way. Eventually I realized their paintings all had something in common that couldn't be attributed to style or technique. The mechanics of painting never change much. We all use our hands and eyes and some painting supplies. Most artists are happy to share their methods. My method is pretty simple. I put green or red where I see green or red, dark or light where I see dark or light and make lots of corrections as I go. The results are predictably ordinary much of the time, but not always.

When I'm painting it feels like I've gotten into a very small boat by myself and pushed off from land out into a vast ocean where there are no fixed points to navigate by and everything's constantly changing. I'm searching for an island in the middle of that ocean where there is a spring with regenerative waters. It's only by being quiet that I can see and feel the subtle signs, the quality of the air and light, the push of the currents on the boat in order to sense where the island lies. The clumsiness of a large boat and the distraction of ideas would blind me. I wouldn't be able to find it. I very often fail to find it anyway and return with nothing more than a documentation of facts I encountered on the way (banal paintings). I can't take anyone with me, and I can only bring back a small amount of water. The only proof I have to offer of that island's existence is the water I bring back for others to drink. The water does what it does for those it works on. My responsibility is just to get into the boat, push off away from land, and try to be quiet. Everything that happens after that is not really up to me. But for the water on that island I'd have no reason to get into the boat. All I know is how I am different as a result of tasting the water. The ultimate worth of all this, like all our actions, is a matter of faith. Once you've made it to that island and tasted the water you're changed. You fall in love with truth. Once you've made a good painting, a beautiful painting, you're driven to try to do it again. There is no longer a choice. All arguments against beauty carry no weight against the experience of it. Reason and intelligence become weightless. Being driven to love truth by experience almost makes me think God/ truth might be good after all, if it weren't for all the people in the world whose experience leads them to prefer illusion. Maybe that's where all the anti-god metaphors come from.

The Oxford dictionary defines *grace* (in Christian belief) as the unmerited favour of God; a divine saving and strengthening influence. It defines *nirvana* (in Buddhism) as perfect bliss and release from karma, attained by the extinction of individuality. These sound very familiar to me. I wonder if they are different interpretations of the same experience.

My painting experiences change from day to day. Sometimes painting is fun and effortless. I can feel charmed, though this always feels a bit fragile. Sometimes painting is a painful struggle that leaves me in despair. Sometimes it's a calm and straightforward activity and doesn't feel fragile at all.

After all these years I'm still not sure that there is a direct correlation between my pleasant and unpleasant painting experiences and whether the resulting painting is worth saving. Sometimes the charmed ones seem insubstantial. Sometimes after years of frustrated attempts a painting defeats me. No matter how often I return to it, I fail and I end up destroying it or turning the panel upside down and painting something completely different on it. There doesn't seem to be any point in planning anything anymore. I never end up doing what I thought I was going to do. No situation is without potential.

What does seem to be common to the paintings worth saving is that at some point in the making of them I get a sense of the end of struggle between myself and everything else. I think that's where the sense of there no longer being a distinct and separate "myself" comes from. The longer this continues the more the painting gets filled up with agreement. The painting goes true. It becomes all right to stop.

What keeps me going through all the uncertainty and periods of failure is the memory of beauty and the knowledge that what I need is always there, waiting. Good happens. When it finally does happen, what seemed impossible one moment becomes the easiest thing in the world the next. Others must have similar experiences. I begin to understand why some of us start to believe in a divine influence, a benevolent and indestructible truth, a universal mind or some inclusive sacredness that fills us with gratitude.

I don't like to talk about technique. It would be misleading to attach too much importance to technique when I've made beautiful drawings scribbling with a charcoal stick for a few minutes…the same technique that usually leaves me with what you'd expect to get scribbling with a charcoal stick for a few minutes.

Inferior tools and materials and clumsy technique can undermine my efforts, yet I know the choice of colours I have on my palette or brushes I use can't save me.

The problem is always my relationship to the materials I happen to have chosen and not the materials themselves. I use a number of techniques but none of them are an answer to solving the problem of beauty.

Technique is a kind of knowledge, a kind of sureness that tends to lure you away from looking and feeling. I have found myself mired in knowledge-as-solution. I'm not sure if I can correctly call the one technique I rely on a technique at all. It's more like an attitude. It's not a secret. I try to stop looking for my voice. I try to stop trying to distinguish myself. I try to give up. I try to stop struggling against something that is incomprehensibly bigger and stronger than I am. I think it's a universal wisdom. The word Islam means submission. In Eastern philosophy we are but leaves on a river. For a person in Alcoholics Anonymous the path to recovery requires the acceptance of a higher power. I see the complex mechanism of experience I was born with, my senses and my mind, as an opening to everything that is, an opening to truth. I just need to listen so I can hear. The word "obey" has a Latin root that means "hear".

When I'm painting, I can become aware of a relationship between what seems like creation and destruction. The two seem to become one, or perhaps neither exist other than as different perspectives on change. It's a fearless state. Things are constantly being "created" and "destroyed", constantly changing.

Sometimes the best art appears to be irreverent and destructive, to be punk. Manet and van Gogh seemed like punks to some of their contemporaries. Their sincerity, seriousness, and sanity were suspect. In time we came to realize how sincere they were and we have grown to trust them. It's tough distinguishing between the good people and bad people if both ignore the laws that people have written. It can make us feel uncomfortable, mistrustful, angry, and at sea. We have never been anywhere other than at sea.

– It's Complicated –

I want so much to trust somebody. All I have is my eyes, ears and time to find out whom I can trust, to discriminate between who might care and who might be looking out for themselves first, whether individually or in groups. I think much of what is admired in the world is admired for being great examples of people overpowering other people. It's taken as a license or even an admirable ambition to control others. "Hell is other people." (Sartre)

Many beautiful artists are vain and ruthless. Many deeply moral artists end up being preachy or sentimental. The elite have opportunities the rest of us don't have and yet they may have no broader sense of responsibility than normal.

We want to be treated as equals. We want special treatment. Nature doesn't endow us all equally with power. We aren't treated equally by those endowed with power. The society we want would have us all equal under the law.

The idea of democracy involves us in a struggle to keep governments responsible to the people. We want the word "person" to mean everybody; not just the powerful but the vulnerable as well. That is the ideal, but the definition of a person is debated and evolves. Before we save anybody, we all want to catch hold of that happiness we pursue. Our happiness (as individuals, classes, sexes, races, etc.) can be threatened, our freedom can be restricted by any decision as to which beings are to be accepted as people, giving them rights equal to our own that are to be enforced by law. This is a world full of vulnerability. The opportunities to save a life are overwhelming.

I see the burning bush. I worship the golden calf.

We all suffer from all manner of normalcy. I'd be a monster without self-repression. We want to be happy. We're clever, aggressive, territorial animals and are driven for the most part by biochemistry and overpowering social and survival instincts. There was hope the ideas that drove the social and technological revolutions would give us the opportunity to become our best selves but we sit in cars at drive-thrus and in chairs staring at screens and allow the means to become the end, the medium to become the message.

Revolutions promise us joy. Our nature remains. We never seem to be up to our dreams, our utopias. We imagine things that require us to be better than we are: Camelot, Star Trek, Marxism, democracy, or feminism.

We get stuck with little-emperor cultures. It's all too complicated to figure out on our own. We long for someone strong. We long for someone who will tell us what is right and what is wrong. We long for someone with a bible, lambs hoping for a shepherd, too often getting a wolf. There will always be people whose success is measured against the subjection and humiliation of others, whose pride in their success is defined by other's failures and whose personal strength is put to use to gain personal exaltation. That is what sustains a perpetual hell on earth, from the ghetto to the shiny towers.

If a person discovers they have personal power, the hardest thing for them is to avoid personal corruption. Media and language have tremendous power. It hurts when Hollywood, or someone as talented as Rubens, uses their power to seduce us like a car commercial. It's scary what you can get people to do, what you can get people to believe. Without beauty life is nasty, brutish and probably too long. We are all equal in at least one respect. We are all fettered by the overwhelming incident of biology. It's a part of truth; a tiny part that appears huge.

– It's Simple –

It isn't wise to use the expression, "The Canon of Great Art," as if critics and scholars, the popes of culture, chose great art. Some of it is what survives by being loved enough to save and recommend. Some of the greatest art lives in the kitchens, resurrected on certain

Saturday nights. It arrives from the infinite, passes through us and returns to the infinite again until the next time we are open. It's a soft thing, easily deflected by an insistent personality. It will sneak up on you when you forget yourself for a moment.

I'm not ashamed to admit that I want to make Great Art. On a number of occasions I've ended up weeping at the experience of beauty. I ask myself why I'm crying. It seems to be from some deep and unexpected sense of relief. I feel delivered from banality, from the sense that no one cares, or from the sense that people's concerns are exclusively worldly. It ends some kind of loneliness. It is redemption from narrowness and subjectivity. The experience is like an embrace where no one and nothing is an outsider. No one is left at a distance from the sacred.

In 2006 I went to visit my daughter, Lucy, who was studying dance in Rotterdam. We went on a day-trip to the Kröller-Müller Museum, the one in the middle of a National

Park in the Netherlands. The museum is famous for its collection of van Gogh paintings. I hadn't been to any world-class art gallery in years. I was nervous that I wouldn't be moved anymore by any so-called great art, nervous that I had become jaded. We were late arriving and only had a short time before the gallery closed, so we headed straight for the rooms with the van Goghs. I remember walking quickly down hallways lined with art and turning a corner to see some of his paintings hanging down the hallway directly in front of me. A smile immediately appeared on my face and it grew as I got closer. I moved from one painting of his to another, quite happy to be there. Eventually I found myself in front of one painting that I wasn't familiar with, though subsequently I realized I had seen it before in a reproduction. I guess it never really did much for me in reproduction. It was one of the wheat field paintings he did at Saint-Rémy. As I stood there with my eyes moving over it, something about it suddenly did something to me. I started to sob—heaving sobs. I had to sit down. People came over to see if I was in distress. I had to take my face out of my hands and look up at them, with tears running down my face and a big smile, and tell them I was just fine.

Thomas Mann's novella, *Death in Venice*, is a cautionary tale about confusing two types of beauty. At the end of the story the author literally points us in the right direction. In attractiveness-type beauty we are left with an ache to possess the object, the form. With truth-type beauty it's only ever joyful. Whoever owns the object or form is irrelevant. It's not the form itself but what is manifested in the form. It's everybody's and nobody's. Maybe it takes possession of you, it breaks your armour and you expand out into it. You participate in the artist's expansiveness. It's unrestrictedly generous.

I want to do this, I want to make beautiful paintings, but I realize I can't get there from here. I can't try and make one. Striving to be great doesn't help. I just need to do my job and hope for the best. Sometimes, strangely enough, in telling myself I'm going to make a bad one on purpose, I can trick myself into avoiding pretentiousness.

A character in Alexander Solzhenitsyn's novel, *One Day in the Life of Ivan Denisovitch*, says "too much art is no art at all." There is an entry in the thesaurus for "artlessness" under which are listed: "ingenuousness, simpleness, naivety, innocence, unguardedness, unpretentiousness, sincerity, trustfullness, openness." All this reminds me of that lovely Shaker song, *Simple Gifts*.

In Shakespeare's play, *The Tempest*, Prospero, the usurped Duke/magician, has, in his daughter Miranda, one gift to bestow. This gift is "plain and holy innocence." Prospero's one great fear is that this gift won't be received with respect. It's a gift that when respected "will outstrip all praise," a gift that if held at a distance by disrespect will issue nothing but "barren hate, sour-eyed disdain and discord."

Plain and holy innocence is the *sine qua non* of beautiful art. With *The Tempest*, Shakespeare passes the torch and includes instructions. Monet and Beethoven made some of their best art late in life. Monet was going blind. Beethoven was going deaf. The world became brave and new for them again. A person's plain and holy innocence can be destroyed but the reason for it to abide is indestructible. If a reason is found that ends innocence, it's reason's failing.

Naiveté and innocence are two different things. When you pay attention, naiveté dies. When you pay attention, innocence grows.

To be intellectually fair to life, we need to acknowledge that our concepts are limited, yet our condition is a consciousness of limitlessness. We have a dictionary full of only words to express things. They offer no way out of that bewildering condition.

To love truth, we have to accept paradox. If you acknowledge that agenda, prejudice, preconception, and conceit are facts of life and therefore facts of art, and then decide that *your* conceit is an art *without* agenda, prejudice, preconception and conceit, you are expecting a lot—sophisticated innocence. It's no wonder that it's so normal to fail.

Sometimes, I think all of Western thought is like God's special child. He pats us on the head and puts our work up on the fridge.

Mythology is our imagination's attempt to get our minds around the most important things. Those most important things become unimportant with our minds around them. Ideas in art should never be more than opportunities to outstrip our ideas. If you're not smart enough to realize that it's not intellect you need to be a good artist, you're not smart enough to be a good artist. Tell intellect you still love it, but you just need to be by yourself for a while.

– A Time to Love –

There is a famous passage in chapter three of Ecclesiastes in the Bible that begins "To every thing there is a season, and a time to every purpose under the heaven." The author goes on to list all the things we spend our time doing, the vanity of it all. One of them is "a time to love." Maybe we love in vain. Maybe, among all the kinds of love that exist, there is one kind that is not in vain.

When I sit on my couch with a cup of tea, looking at a book of Monet's paintings or reading George Eliot's *Middlemarch*, and come to feel life is good, will that be enough? Once my tea is finished and it's time to do something, will I be compelled to try and make my own actions beautiful?

We're proud of people like Picasso. Some are even proud of people like Napoleon, all that strutting and fretting we do. In that fact about human nature we find the cause of our tragic human folly. It's completely understandable, natural even, that we would be proud. It's as a result of those traits, those skills, those abilities that we survive as a species, that we adapt and continue to thrive. We praise the strongest, the cleverest, the creative ones. We aspire to those traits. We seek to mate with those displaying those traits. We follow them and are proud.

The history of humans is the history of the failure of ideas. In studying history we hear the haunting refrain "never again, never again, never again." The critical stance we adopt with respect to what we perceive as wrong is born of the conceit that we know better, the same conceit that gets us into trouble in the first place. Even in pointing out that with the nuclear weapons that have been amassed the surface of the earth could be altered until it becomes unrecognizable, we can't help saying it with our chests puffed out a bit. There is no solution to this. It's what we are, natural beings obeying natural laws.

Atoms of hydrogen, oxygen, carbon, etc. organized themselves into a complex that became aware of itself, saw the moon, dreamed of going there and did. Somehow

I get the feeling it was inevitable. We are complex. Culture and technology represent increases in the intrinsic complexity of things. The origins of complexity will remain mysterious. Our experience of phenomena is consistent, but we can't know why it's consistently "this," instead of consistently "that," not consistent at all, or simply absent. Every new light we turn on reveals a greater depth to the darkness in which all we can do is imagine gods and monsters, or more light bulbs. We stand on a rock for a while breathing, in the middle of something, watching our pyramids crumble around us.

The ambition to be beautiful is really an anti-ambition. It's the ambition to de-create the self.

Ultimately, it's about love. The physical universe is indifferent to suffering. We have no claim to kindness but I listen to Bach's music and I find myself among the beloved. I don't know if I'm supposed to thank Bach or truth.

In the ancient Greek play, *Antigone*, Sophocles warns us to beware of hubris and to always hold the gods in awe. The hardest thing an artist can do, the hardest thing a person can do, is act without self-interest.

When old age shall this generation waste,
Thou shalt remain, in midst of other woe
Than ours, a friend to man, to whom thou
sayst, "Beauty is truth, truth beauty"—that is all
Ye know on earth and all ye need to know.

–John Keats, *"Ode on a Grecian Urn"*

In spite of what it seems like I've tried to do here, beauty doesn't need to be defended. It's just something that is. It's just something that happens. If something is to be found guilty before a court of humankind, it's human pride. If beauty has a role in that court, it's as mercy. We have no claim to kindness—and yet, there it is. It's beauty that saves us from Sartre's "L'enfer, c'est les autres." Perhaps this is what Dostoevsky meant when he had Prince Myshkin, the central character in his novel *The Idiot*, claim that beauty will save the world.

The last lines of George Eliot's novel *Middlemarch* refer to the novel's selfless character Dorothea.

> *But the effect of her being on those around her was incalculably diffusive: for the growing good of the world is partly dependent on unhistoric acts; and that things are not so ill with you and me as they might have been, is half owing to the number who lived faithfully a hidden life, and rest in unvisited tombs.*

When Nelson Mandela came out of prison after twenty-seven years and found himself in a position of power, he took no revenge. Sometimes beauty is historic.

It might be fair to put it something like this. The absence of beauty in a person is the root of callous indifference. The presence of beauty is the proof of love. The presence of it in what we've done is the great value of art.

Nobody can be good all the time, but if I can be good while I'm painting, at least that's something, a few shining moments.

Stephen May
Fredericton
2011-2018

Acknowledgements

I owe so much to so many, some living and some dead. I'd like to thank my parents, Marilyn and Larry May, for too many things to list; Marnie Pomeroy for endless encouragement, many great conversations over many years, and for all her warnings about bad writing, some of which I'll probably regret not heeding, like run-on sentences; Nancy Bauer for more conversations, genuine interest and a perfect Foreword; Alan Hall for initiating the whole thing by asking me to come to his philosophy class and talk about being an artist—it's his fault really; George Strunz for thinking there was something in the early versions of this essay worth sharing; Keith Helmuth for thinking it was worth publishing, for all his question marks, and for saving the reader from a lot of bad writing; Brendan Helmuth for a sensitive and thoughtful design; my daughter Lucy for the heated arguments about our art and life convictions (Lucy and my other daughter, Claire are my other great privilege); Inge Pataki and Germaine Pataki-Thériault of Gallery 78 for their faith in art and their willingness to trust me; friends Alex, Les, Kim, Neil and all the staff at the Fredericton Public Library for "tech support"; and all the artists and other people, living and dead, who continue to save me.

About the Author

Stephen May was born in Témiscaming, Quebec in 1957. He enrolled in the Photographic Arts Program at Ryerson Polytechnical Institute in 1976, and later attended art classes at the Ottawa School of Art. In 1979 he enrolled at Mount Allison University and graduated with a Bachelor of Fine Arts degree in 1983.

He then traveled throughout Europe in order to immerse himself in various collections of great art. On return to Canada, Stephen took up residence in Fredericton. He obtained a seasonal position with Theatre New Brunswick as a prop builder, which gave him five months a year to devote to painting. In 1992 he was awarded a Canada Council grant enabling him to take a year's sabbatical from Theatre New Brunswick during which he concentrated on his painting. This step launched Stephen into painting full-time, at which he has continued to be successful.

In subsequent years, Stephen has had numerous public exhibits and has been active in the local arts community. He is professionally represented by Gallery 78 in Fredericton. A selection of his work can be viewed at www.gallery78.com/artists/stephen-may

The Beaverbrook Art Gallery in Fredericton has purchased his work for its permanent collection. In 2006, the Beaverbrook mounted a solo retrospective, *Stephen May: Embodiments*. In 2007, he was awarded the prestigious *Miller Brittain Award for Excellence in the Visual Arts.*